MINNESOTA

The North Star State

BY
JOHN HAMILTON

Abdo & Daughters
An imprint of Abdo Publishing | abdopublishing.com

abdopublishing.com

Published by ABDO Publishing, a division of ABDO, PO Box 398166, Minneapolis, Minnesota 55439. Copyright © 2017 by Abdo Consulting Group, Inc. International copyrights reserved in all countries. No part of this book may be reproduced in any form without written permission from the publisher. ABDO & Daughters™ is a trademark and logo of ABDO Publishing.

Printed in the United States of America, North Mankato, Minnesota.
032016
092016

Editor: Sue Hamilton   **Contributing Editor:** Bridget O'Brien
Graphic Design: Sue Hamilton
Cover Art Direction: Candice Keimig   **Cover Photo Selection:** Neil Klinepier
Cover Photo: iStock
Interior Images: Alamy, AP, Corbis, Como Zoo, David Olson, Dreamstime, Getty Images, Glow Images, Government of Ontario Art Collection, Granger, Gunter Kuchler, Haikiba, History in Full Color-Restoration/Colorization, Hull-Rust-Mahoning Mine, iStock, John Hamilton, Library of Congress, Mall of America, Minden Pictures, Mile High Maps, Minnesota Historical Society, Minnesota Lynx, Minnesota Secretary of State, Minnesota State Fair, Minnesota Timberwolves, Minnesota Twins, Minnesota Vikings, Minnesota Wild, Minnesota Zoo, Mountain High Maps, National Park Service, Nic Ebinger, Science Museum of Minnesota, Seth Eastman, St. Olaf College, U.S. Bank, U.S. Dept of State, U.S. Navy, University of Minnesota, Visit Duluth, and Wikimedia.

Statistics: *State and City Populations*, U.S. Census Bureau, July 1, 2015/2014 estimates; *Land and Water Area*, U.S. Census Bureau, 2010 Census, MAF/TIGER database; *State Temperature Extremes*, NOAA National Climatic Data Center; *Climatology and Average Annual Precipitation*, NOAA National Climatic Data Center, 1980-2015 statewide averages; *State Highest and Lowest Points*, NOAA National Geodetic Survey.

Websites: To learn more about the United States, visit booklinks.abdopublishing.com. These links are routinely monitored and updated to provide the most current information available.

Cataloging-in-Publication Data

Names: Hamilton, John, 1959- author.
Title: Minnesota / by John Hamilton.
Description: Minneapolis, MN : Abdo Publishing, [2017] | Series: The United States of America | Includes index.
Identifiers: LCCN 2015957616 | ISBN 9781680783254 (lib. bdg.) | ISBN 9781680774290 (ebook)
Subjects: LCSH: Minnesota--Juvenile literature.
Classification: DDC 977.6--dc23
LC record available at http://lccn.loc.gov/2015957616

CONTENTS

THE NORTH STAR STATE

Minnesota is larger than life, like the mythical lumberjack Paul Bunyan. The state's motto is *L'Etoile du Nord,* which is French for "The Star of the North." That is why Minnesota's nickname is "The North Star State." It harkens back to the days of French *voyageurs* paddling across Minnesota's wilderness lakes. Today, fur trapping and logging have been replaced by agriculture and bustling cities. The craggy North Shore of Lake Superior shares the spotlight with the Twin Cities and the Mall of America. But it is still Minnesota's natural beauty that draws the most visitors to the state each year.

Sometimes quirky, always hardy, Minnesotans love trendy cafes and rock bands as well as ice fishing and corn mazes. Quick to lend a helping hand, Minnesota is a top-ranked state for volunteering. And no matter what the season—from bone-chilling winters to pleasant summers—Minnesota Nice is always on full display.

The Spoonbridge and Cherry *sculpture is outside Minneapolis's Walker Art Center. The sculpture is nearly 52 feet (16 m) long.*

QUICK FACTS

Name: Minnesota's name probably comes from a Dakota Native American word, *Mnisota*, which means "clear water." However, it might also translate to "cloudy water," which refers to the morning mist rising over the state's lakes and valleys.

State Capital: St. Paul, population 297,640

Date of Statehood: May 11, 1858 (32nd state)

Population: 5,489,594 (21st-most populous state)

Area (Total Land and Water): 86,936 square miles (225,163 sq km), 12th-largest state

Largest City: Minneapolis, population 407,207

Nickname: The North Star State; the Land of 10,000 Lakes; the Gopher State

Motto: *L'Etoile du Nord* (The Star of the North)

State Bird: Common Loon

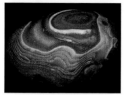

State Flower: Showy Lady's Slipper

State Gemstone: Lake Superior Agate

State Tree: Red (Norway) Pine

State Song: "Hail! Minnesota"

Highest Point: Eagle Mountain, 2,301 feet (701 m)

Lowest Point: Lake Superior, 601 feet (183 m)

Average July High Temperature: 81°F (27°C)

Record High Temperature: 115°F (46°C), in Beardsley on July 29, 1917

Average January Low Temperature: 0°F (-18°C)

Record Low Temperature: -60°F (-51°C), in Tower on February 2, 1996

Average Annual Precipitation: 28 inches (71 cm)

Number of U.S. Senators: 2

Number of U.S. Representatives: 8

U.S. Postal Service Abbreviation: MN

GEOGRAPHY

Minnesota is in the Upper Midwest. It is the northernmost state in the contiguous United States. Its land and water area is 86,936 square miles (225,163 sq km). That makes it the 12th-largest state.

Many volcanic and metamorphic rocks, such as granite and gneiss, are found in northern Minnesota. Some are nearly 3.6 billion years old. They are among the oldest rocks found on Earth. Huge deposits of iron ore also formed in the north, between 1.6-2.5 billion years ago. In southern Minnesota, fossil evidence of ancient seabeds is found in the sedimentary rock.

About 12,000 years ago, ice sheets more than 1-mile (1.6-km) thick scoured the landscape. When these Ice Age glaciers melted, they left behind fertile soil, deep river valleys, and thousands of lakes.

Minnesota is filled with thousands of lakes.

Minnesota's total land and water area is 86,936 square miles (225,163 sq km). It is the 12th-largest state. The state capital is St. Paul.

Minnesota is nicknamed the "Land of 10,000 Lakes," but if one counts all the lakes that are bigger than 10 acres (4 ha), there are 11,842! Minnesota's northeastern tip (called the Arrowhead region) borders Lake Superior, the largest freshwater lake in the world. Large lakes that are completely within Minnesota's borders include Red, Mille Lacs, and Leech Lakes. Lake Minnetonka is the largest lake in the Twin Cities metropolitan area.

Split Rock Lighthouse overlooks Lake Superior.

Minnesota has more than 69,000 miles (111,045 km) of rivers and streams. The mighty Mississippi River gets its start in Minnesota, at Lake Itasca. It winds its way southward for more than 680 miles (1,094 km) through the state. Other major rivers include the Minnesota and St. Croix Rivers. The Red River forms most of Minnesota's western border with North Dakota. It flows northward into Canada.

Because it is such a large state, there are many kinds of biomes in Minnesota. Coniferous forests of pine, fir, and spruce trees are in the north. In the south are deciduous woodlands and gently rolling hills. Prairie grasslands can be found in western Minnesota.

Much of Minnesota has been set aside as wilderness. Along the Canadian border are the Boundary Waters Canoe Area Wilderness and Voyageurs National Park. In addition, scattered all over Minnesota are 67 state parks, 58 state forests, and 7 state recreation areas. Minnesota's first state park was created in 1891 at Lake Itasca.

Boundary Waters Canoe Area Wilderness

CLIMATE AND WEATHER

Minnesota has a continental climate, thanks to its location near the center of North America. In general, summers are hot, while winters are cold. However, there are big regional differences. In the north, summers are shorter and cooler. In the south, summers are longer and more humid. The growing season is about 160 days in the southeast, but averages just 90 days in the north.

Minnesota is famous for its extreme weather. The state can be struck by blinding blizzards that dump three feet (.9 m) or more of snow, or rumbling thunderstorms that bring golf-ball-sized hail. Situated on the northern edge of Tornado Alley, the state averages about 27 twisters per year. However, on most days in Minnesota the weather is surprisingly pleasant. People enjoy outdoor activities throughout the year.

A car drives through a "whiteout" during a severe Minnesota snowstorm.

Minnesota's average July high temperature is 81°F (27°C). In January, the average low temperature is 0°F (-18°C). Minnesota winters are notorious for their cold snaps. On February 2, 1996, the thermometer sank to a record low of -60°F (-51°C) in the northern Minnesota town of Tower.

On most days in Minnesota the weather is surprisingly pleasant. People enjoy outdoor activities throughout the year.

PLANTS AND
ANIMALS

Forestland covers about 17.3 million acres (7 million ha) of Minnesota. That is about one third of the state. In the north and northeast are vast coniferous forests. The most common trees include pine, fir, spruce, aspen, and birch. Red pine is the official state tree. Also called Norway pine, it normally grows up to 80 feet (24 m) tall and has reddish bark when it matures.

Minnesota has huge numbers of deciduous trees. They lose their leaves at the end of the growing season. Minnesota's deciduous forest biome is a wide diagonal band stretching across the state. It starts in the southeast and extends all the way to the northwest. Common broadleaf trees include sugar maple, oak, cottonwood, ash, elm, and aspen.

A red squirrel climbs down a red pine tree in Minnesota.

When settlers first arrived in southwestern Minnesota, there were almost 18 million acres (7.3 million ha) of prairie grasslands. Today, most of that has been turned into farmland.

Minnesota's state flower is the showy lady's slipper. These pink-and-white orchids are very rare. They are found in swamps or bogs. Minnesota is the only state to have an orchid as its official flower.

A pheasant takes flight to escape a fox on a Minnesota prairie.

Timber Wolf

Large mammals found in Minnesota's forests and prairies include white-tailed deer, black bears, moose, elk, foxes, cougars, beavers, bobcats, and coyotes. There are many gray wolves, also called timber wolves, in central and northern Minnesota. Alaska is the only state with a bigger gray wolf population.

Smaller mammals found scampering in Minnesota's woodlands and prairies include squirrels, chipmunks, minks, moles, porcupines, raccoons, river otters, shrews, skunks, and weasels. Gophers are especially common everywhere except northeastern Minnesota. This 11-inch (28-cm) rodent is the mascot for the University of Minnesota (the "Golden Gophers").

Minnesota is along the Mississippi Flyway. It is the path many birds take when migrating north or south. Because of this, the state sees many ducks and Canada geese flying overhead. Other common birds spotted in Minnesota include crows, mourning doves, American robins, cardinals, blue jays, and chickadees.

Red-Tailed Hawk

Raptors include bald eagles, red-tailed hawks, falcons, and many species of owls. Popular game birds include ring-necked pheasants, ducks, grouse, and wild turkeys. The common loon is Minnesota's official state bird. Its haunting wail is often heard on wilderness lakes in the early morning or late evening.

Minnesota is an angler's paradise. Lurking under the waves of the state's thousands of lakes and streams are 158 species of fish. The official state fish is the walleye, the most prized catch for Minnesota anglers. Other popular catches include trout, bass, muskellunge, northern pike, salmon, lake sturgeon, sunfish, perch, and crappie.

An angler holds up a largemouth bass.

PLANTS AND ANIMALS

HISTORY

About 11,000 years ago, Paleo-Indians arrived in today's Minnesota. They were the ancestors of modern Native Americans. They used spears to hunt mammoths and large bison. They also gathered plants for food, and made copper tools such as knives and fishhooks.

In time, the native peoples built permanent settlements. They used bows and arrows to hunt, and some learned to harvest wild rice in the marshes of northern Minnesota. Others built large earthen mounds for religious purposes, such as burying their dead.

French explorers arrived in the 1600s. By that time, the area was settled by the Dakotas, a Native American tribe also called the Sioux. Soon, another tribe migrated from the east. They were the Ojibwe, also called the Chippewa. They clashed with the Dakota people. Eventually, the Dakotas were forced out of the region.

The French were interested in Minnesota because it was filled with fur-bearing animals such as beavers and foxes. Beaver pelts were especially valuable. They were prized in Europe for making hats. Soon, French *voyageurs* were paddling huge canoes loaded with furs across Minnesota's waterways. Many people made fortunes in the fur trade.

Father Louis Hennepin explored the Minnesota area in 1680. He saw spectacular waterfalls that he named St. Anthony Falls.

Catholic priest Father Louis Hennepin was a member of a French expedition exploring Minnesota in 1680. Along the Mississippi River, he witnessed waterfalls that he estimated were 50 feet (15 m) tall. He named them St. Anthony Falls. Today, the falls are located near downtown Minneapolis.

The fur trade continued to grow. Great Britain competed with France for the best fur-trapping territory. After the French and Indian War (1754-1763), the victorious British took over most of present-day Minnesota.

In 1765, the North West Company built a trading post at Grand Portage, on the far eastern tip of northern Minnesota. It became a major business center for trappers and Ojibwe Native Americans.

After the United States won independence from Great Britain in 1783, much of the eastern half of Minnesota became part of the Northwest Territory. Most of the land west of the Mississippi River was bought from France in 1803 as part of the Louisiana Purchase.

In 1825, the United States Army finished construction of Fort Snelling. The stone-walled fort rests atop a bluff overlooking the place where the Mississippi and Minnesota Rivers meet, near present-day Minneapolis and St. Paul. Fort Snelling protected the important waterways. It was also a place where fur trappers, farmers, and Native Americans could trade and do business. Soon, flour mills sprang up at nearby St. Anthony Falls, and families began building homes and farms in the area.

In 1825, the United States Army built Fort Snelling near present-day Minneapolis and St. Paul. It became a busy business and meeting place.

By the 1830s, the demand for fur shrank. Other industries became more important to Minnesota's economy. They included farming, mining, and lumber.

Minnesota Territory was created in 1849 as more people moved into the area. On May 11, 1858, Minnesota became the 32nd state to join the Union. The first governor was Henry H. Sibley.

In 1861, the country was plunged into the bloody Civil War (1861-1865). Minnesota was the first state to volunteer troops for the anti-slavery Union. More than 26,000 Minnesotans fought against the Southern Confederacy.

During the 1860s, thousands of immigrants settled in Minnesota. Many received 160 acres (65 ha) of free farmland, thanks to the Homestead Act of 1862. Many of the newcomers were from Scandinavia and Germany.

The Second Minnesota Regiment fought in the Civil War at Tennessee's Battle of Missionary Ridge on November 25, 1863.

The hanging of 38 Dakota Native Americans on December 26, 1862, was the largest mass execution in United States history.

In August 1862, fighting broke out between settlers and Dakota Native Americans. The Dakota were angry because of broken treaties and mistreatment. The Dakota War of 1862 (also called the Sioux Uprising of 1862) caused the deaths of hundreds of soldiers, settlers, and Native Americans. After the war, most of the Dakota were forced out of Minnesota, and 38 were hanged for war crimes in the city of Mankato.

In the last half of the 1900s, new industries came to Minnesota. The state became a center for health care, education, and high technology companies, especially computers and electronics. Agriculture continued to be a big part of the economy, even as many small family-owned farms gave way to larger, company farms.

DID YOU KNOW?

• Paul Bunyan is a folklore giant who got his start in the logging camps of the northeast, especially Maine. When loggers arrived in Minnesota in the 1800s, Paul came with them. Many tall tales were told of the oversized lumberjack who could fell an entire forest with a single swing of his mighty ax. In 1937, the city of Bemidji built an 18-foot (5-m) tall statue of the "King of the Lumberjacks." Standing next to him is his companion, Babe the Blue Ox.

• On September 7, 1876, eight men wearing linen dusters rode their horses into the town of Northfield, Minnesota. They were members of the James-Younger Gang, led by the notorious outlaw Jesse James. They entered the First National Bank and tried unsuccessfully to rob it. Instead, the gang found itself in a gunfight with the townsfolk. Two Northfield citizens and two bandits were killed. After a two-week chase through southern Minnesota, four other gang members were either killed or captured. Only Jesse and his brother Frank escaped.

• The Hull-Rust-Mahoning Mine is in Hibbing, Minnesota, in the state's Mesabi Iron Range region. It is one of the largest open-pit iron mines in the world. First opened in 1895, the mine is now more than 3 miles (5 km) long, 1 mile (1.6 km) wide, and 535 feet (163 m) deep. More than 690 million tons (626 million metric tons) of iron ore has been dug out of the mine.

• On September 1, 1894, a huge fire engulfed the northern Minnesota logging town of Hinckley and the surrounding area. Fueled by forest debris and a long drought, the firestorm burned more than 250,000 acres (101,171 ha) of land in just four hours. At least 418 people were killed, and Hinckley was burned to the ground. In 1918, an even deadlier fire scorched much of the town of Cloquet and Carlton County. The inferno killed 453 people, destroyed 38 communities, and left thousands homeless. It was the deadliest natural disaster in Minnesota history.

• The Armistice Day Blizzard struck Minnesota on November 11, 1940. The day started warm, but then the weather rapidly changed. Temperatures unexpectedly sank to below freezing. Heavy snow and high winds made travel impossible. Many people were surprised by the storm, and 49 Minnesotans were killed.

DID YOU KNOW?

PEOPLE

Charles Lindbergh (1902-1974) was a pilot, inventor, and author. In 1927, he flew his single-engine plane, *Spirit of St. Louis*, across the Atlantic Ocean. It was the first time anyone had flown solo across the ocean. He flew nonstop for 33.5 hours from Long Island, New York, to an airfield near Paris, France. "Lucky Lindy" was just 25 when he made the dangerous 3,600-mile (5,794-km) journey.

After his historic flight, Lindbergh became a celebrity. He helped improve the United States Air Mail Service. His fame took a tragic turn in 1932 when kidnappers murdered his baby son, Charles.

During World War II, Lindbergh helped the military improve its aircraft. He also flew many combat missions. In 1953, his book, *The Spirit of St. Louis*, won a Pulitzer Prize. Lindbergh grew up in Little Falls, Minnesota.

Hubert H. Humphrey (1911-1978) was the vice president of the United States, serving under President Lyndon Johnson from 1965-1969. He represented Minnesota for many years as a United States senator, and was also the mayor of Minneapolis. Humphrey was a strong liberal Democrat who wanted to abolish racial discrimination. While in Congress, he had a major role in passing the Civil Rights Act of 1964.

Walter "Fritz" Mondale (1928-) was vice president of the United States from 1977-1981, serving under President Jimmy Carter. Before that, he was a United States senator for the state of Minnesota for 12 years. Mondale was a Democrat who supported tax reform, fair housing, and civil rights. In 1984, he ran for president but lost to Ronald Reagan. Afterwards, he served as the United States ambassador to Japan. Mondale was born in Ceylon, Minnesota.

Lindsey Vonn (1984-) is a world-champion ski racer. She has won four World Cup overall championships, plus dozens of World Cup races during her career. She is one of only six women to win all five World Cup race events, including super-G, slalom, giant slalom, downhill, and super combined. At the 2010 Winter Olympic Games in British Columbia, Canada, she became the first woman to win a gold medal in the downhill event. Vonn was born in St. Paul, Minnesota.

Bob Dylan (1941-) is a very popular and influential singer, songwriter, poet, and author. He became famous during the civil rights and anti-war movements of the 1960s with such folk songs as "Blowin' in the Wind" and "The Times They Are a-Changin'." His long, award-winning career has spanned many musical styles, including pop, jazz, country, and blues. He has sold more than 100 million records. Dylan was born in Duluth, Minnesota, but spent much of his childhood in Hibbing.

Prince (1958-2016) was a Minneapolis-born musician, songwriter, music producer, and actor. His full name was Prince Rogers Nelson. Skilled at playing many instruments, he was one of the pioneers of the "Minneapolis sound," a combination of rock, funk, and pop. His most popular albums included *Purple Rain*, *1999*, *Graffiti Bridge*, and many others. He sold more than 100 million records in his lifetime. He recorded music at his Paisley Park Studio in Chanhassen, Minnesota.

Charles Schulz (1922-2000) was a cartoonist most famous for his *Peanuts* comic strip. He was born in Minneapolis, but grew up in neighboring St. Paul. Schulz worked as an art teacher before his comics became popular in the 1950s. Readers all over America delighted in Charlie Brown, his dog Snoopy, and all the *Peanuts* gang. Schulz won many awards for his work, including the United States Congressional Gold Medal. His work strongly influenced many other comic artists.

CITIES

Minneapolis

Minneapolis is the largest city in Minnesota. Its population is 407,207. Across the Mississippi River to the east is **St. Paul**. It is the capital of Minnesota, with a population of 297,640. Because they are so close, Minneapolis and St. Paul are called the Twin Cities. Together with their suburbs, the sprawling urban area is home to more than 3.8 million people.

Minneapolis is a major Midwestern business center. There are many banking, health care, transportation, and technology businesses. The city is famous for its many parks, including Minnehaha Falls and Lake Calhoun. It is also well known for its music, theater, and visual arts communities, including the world-famous Guthrie Theater.

Minneapolis is often ranked as one of the fittest cities in the country, with many dedicated running and biking paths. The city's hospitals are among the best in the nation. There are also many universities and colleges. The University of Minnesota's main campus has more than 50,000 students.

St. Paul

Science Museum of Minnesota

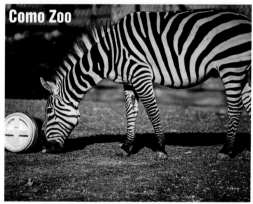
Como Zoo

Although Minneapolis is more well known, the state capital of St. Paul has its own exciting atmosphere. Major employers include government, health care, education, finance, and telecommunications. Favorite attractions include the Como Zoo, the Science Museum of Minnesota, Fort Snelling State Park, the Minnesota History Center, and the Minnesota Children's Museum.

The St. Paul Winter Carnival began in 1886. Each year, the festival's ice sculptures, parades, sledding, and treasure hunt attract more than 350,000 visitors.

CITIES

Above: *The Duluth Lakewalk path borders Lake Superior and the city's downtown.* **Right:** *A ship travels under the Aerial Lift Bridge.*

Duluth rests on the southwestern tip of Lake Superior. Its population is 86,238. It is one of the busiest ports in the country. During the summer shipping season, huge cargo vessels transport millions of tons of grain, iron ore, coal, and other goods through the port. The city has many historical buildings. The Canal Park waterfront district is a popular tourist destination. It includes the city's Aerial Lift Bridge, the Great Lakes Aquarium, and the *William A. Irwin*, a retired Great Lakes freighter that is now a floating museum.

Rochester is a southern Minnesota city that is home to the world-famous Mayo Clinic. The clinic was founded in 1889 by Dr. William W. Mayo and his two sons, William J. and Charles Mayo. Today, the world-renowned medical center is home to 4,200 doctors and scientists. Besides health care, other major businesses in the city include computer manufacturing, food processing, and retail. Silver Lake is famous for attracting large flocks of Canada geese. Rochester's population is 111,402.

Charles H. and William J. Mayo

TRANSPORTATION

Early in Minnesota's history, canoes were important for moving furs to far-off trading posts. Today, modern 1,000-foot (305-m) cargo vessels carry huge loads of iron ore and grain across Lake Superior to cities along the Great Lakes. The Mississippi River is also an important waterway. Barges transport grain and other bulky products all the way to and from the Gulf of Mexico.

A ship loaded with taconite iron ore pellets leaves from Two Harbors, Minnesota.

Minnesota has 18 railroad companies hauling freight on 4,450 miles (7,162 km) of track across the state. The most common products carried by rail include metallic ores, grains, and other farm products. Sand and chemicals are also often hauled by rail. Amtrak's *Empire Builder* carries passengers from Winona in the southeast, through the Twin Cities, and onward to Fargo in the northwest.

There are 138,767 miles (223,324 km) of public roadways in Minnesota. Major interstate highways include I-35, I-90, and I-94. Trucks use a network of state highways to haul grains and other products from farming communities to markets in larger cities.

Minnesota's biggest airport is Minneapolis-St. Paul International Airport. It is one of the busiest airports in the country, handling more than 33 million passengers each year. Other major airports in the state include Duluth International Airport and Rochester International Airport.

In 2015, Minneapolis-St. Paul International Airport was named one of the best airports in the nation by Travel & Leisure *magazine.*

TRANSPORTATION

NATURAL
RESOURCES

Minnesota has millions of acres of rich farmland, especially in the southern part of the state. There are about 74,000 farms statewide.

In the early 1800s, wheat farms and mills made Minnesota a world leader in flour production. Today, wheat is still important, but the biggest money-making crops are corn and soybeans. Most of the corn is used to feed livestock and to make ethanol fuel. However, Minnesota is also a leading state in making canned sweet corn. Other important crops include green peas, sugar beets, oats, beans, potatoes, sunflowers, barley, and hay. There are many apple orchards in southern Minnesota.

Turkeys are the top livestock animals in Minnesota, followed by broiler chickens and hogs. Dairy cows are raised in the hilly, wooded areas of east-central and southeastern Minnesota.

Corn is harvested on a Minnesota farm.

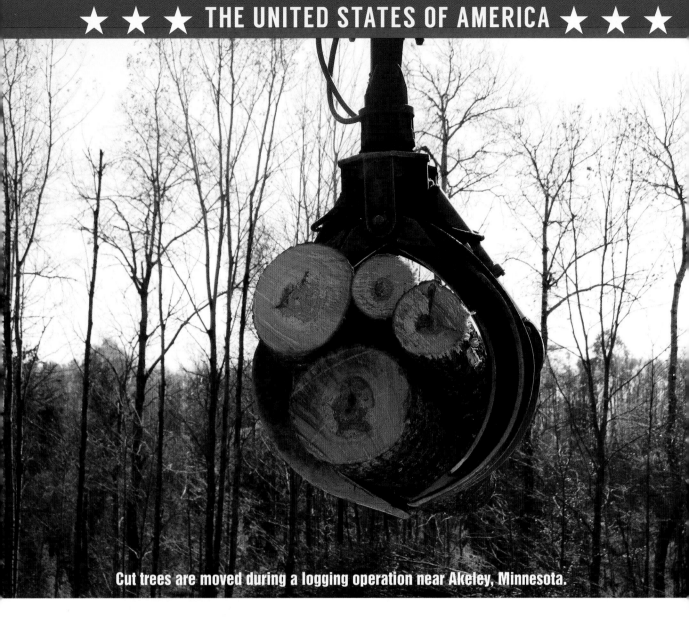

Cut trees are moved during a logging operation near Akeley, Minnesota.

About 34 percent of Minnesota is forested. That is more than 17 million acres (6.9 million ha). Logging was once the most important industry in Minnesota. However, production peaked in the early 1900s and has declined ever since. Limited logging continues in northeastern Minnesota. Pine, spruce, and aspen are used in mills to make paper and pulpwood products.

Minnesota is the nation's top producer of iron ore. Other minerals mined in the state include granite, limestone, silica sand, plus sand and gravel.

NATURAL RESOURCES

INDUSTRY

Manufacturing is the backbone of Minnesota's economy. It adds more than 805,000 jobs and earns about $44 billion yearly. Top industries include computers, electronics, processed foods, machinery, fabricated metals, and medical devices. The 3M Company is based in Maplewood, Minnesota. It makes thousands of products, including the familiar Scotch Brand Tape and Post-it Notes.

Minnesota is a leader in biosciences. It is also a top state for wind energy production. Other important industries include banking, insurance, medical technology, aerospace, and defense. Many big retail companies have their headquarters in Minnesota, including Target and Best Buy.

Best Buy has its headquarters in Richfield, Minnesota.

Minnesota's Mall of America is one of the most visited tourist destinations in the country. About 40 million people visit each year.

Minnesota has a reputation as one of the best places to receive health care. Each year, more than one million people from around the world seek medical treatment at Rochester's Mayo Clinic. Other top hospitals include Abbott Northwestern Hospital and the University of Minnesota Medical Center, both in Minneapolis.

Tourism is big business in Minnesota. People enjoy exploring the state's unspoiled wilderness areas, especially the beautiful lakes of northern Minnesota. They also like the shops, museums, and sporting events in the Twin Cities. Tourism adds about $13.6 billion to Minnesota's economy each year, and supports more than 250,000 jobs. Summer and winter are the most popular times to visit the state.

SPORTS

The Minnesota Vikings play in the U.S. Bank Stadium.

Minnesota has several professional major league sports teams. The Minnesota Vikings play in the National Football League. They have made four Super Bowl appearances. The Minnesota Twins are a Major League Baseball team. They have won the World Series twice, in 1987 and 1991.

The Minnesota Wild skate in the National Hockey League. The Minnesota Timberwolves play in the National Basketball Association. The Minnesota Lynx play in the Women's National Basketball Association. They have won three WNBA Championships.

There are many minor league professional teams representing various sports, including soccer, lacrosse, hockey, and baseball. College sports are also big in Minnesota. The University of Minnesota Golden Gophers have won many national championships in a variety of sports. Hockey, basketball, and football are especially popular.

Minnesotans love the great outdoors. Hiking and hunting are favorite activities. With almost 12,000 lakes in the state, many people enjoy water sports. Waterskiing was invented in Lake City's Lake Pepin in the 1920s. Swimming, boating, sailing, and canoeing are also big. But it is fishing that attracts thousands of people to the lakes each year.

Winter does not stop Minnesotans from enjoying sports. When the lakes freeze over, ice fishing becomes a favorite pastime. Other popular winter sports include downhill and cross-country skiing, snowmobiling, ice skating, dogsledding, and pond hockey.

SPORTS

ENTERTAINMENT

Minnesotans strongly support the performing arts, especially theater. The Guthrie Theater in Minneapolis is acclaimed for producing classic stage plays.

The Walker Art Center in Minneapolis is one of the top modern art museums in the country. Nearby is the Minneapolis Sculpture Garden, which features the famous *Spoonbridge and Cherry* fountain sculpture. The Weisman Art Museum is a landmark on the University of Minnesota main campus. The Minneapolis Institute of Art opened in 1915. It contains more than 80,000 masterpieces of fine art, and admission is always free.

The Minnesota Zoo and the Como Zoo are both in the Twin Cities. The Lake Superior Zoo and the Great Lakes Aquarium are in Duluth.

The Minnesota State Fair is called "The Great Minnesota Get-Together."

The St. Paul Chamber Orchestra and the Minnesota Orchestra are nationally recognized classical music venues. First Avenue, in downtown Minneapolis, is a trendsetting spot for rock bands.

For those who love to shop, the Mall of America in Bloomington has hundreds of shops and enough space to fit nearly 85 football fields.

There are hundreds of fairs and festivals held throughout Minnesota. The Minnesota State Fair attracts hundreds of thousands of visitors each year. The state's biggest amusement park is Valleyfair in Shakopee.

ENTERTAINMENT

TIMELINE

9000 BC—Paleo-Indians first settle into the area known today as Minnesota.

1600s—French fur trappers and traders explore the Lake Superior region.

1680—Father Hennepin witnesses St. Anthony Falls.

1765—The North West Company establishes a trading post at Grand Portage.

1820—The first flour mills are built at St. Anthony Falls.

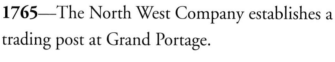

1825—Fort Snelling is completed. Soldiers, settlers, fur traders, and Native Americans conduct business.

1858—Minnesota becomes the 32nd state in the Union.

1862—The Homestead Act gives settlers free land in Minnesota.

1862—The Dakota War of 1862 breaks out. Many settlers and Native Americans are killed.

1876—The James-Younger Gang raids the First National Bank in Northfield.

1918—Fire destroys the town of Cloquet and much of the surrounding area, killing 453 in the deadliest natural disaster in Minnesota history.

1940—The Armistice Day Blizzard kills 49 people.

1941—The first American shots of World War II are fired by a Minnesotan on the USS *Ward*.

1978—The Minnesota Zoo opens in Apple Valley.

1991—The Minnesota Twins win their second World Series championship.

1992—The Mall of America, the largest enclosed shopping mall in the United States, opens in Bloomington.

2006—The Guthrie Theater opens in a new location on the banks of the Mississippi River.

2007—The I-35W bridge collapses into the Mississippi River, killing 13 people.

2015—The Minnesota Lynx win their third Women's National Basketball Association Championship.

GLOSSARY

Biome

A large area containing a community of similar kinds of plants and animals that have traits in common with similar biomes in other parts of the world. Tropical rainforests or deciduous forests are examples of biomes.

Blizzard

A severe winter storm that can be deadly. A blizzard has freezing temperatures, strong winds, blowing snow, and low visibility. Originally, a blizzard was a military term that referred to a musket volley. In the 1870s, the term was applied to severe snowstorms.

Deciduous Woodlands

An area between the northern deciduous forests and prairies of Minnesota. It is an area rich with trees such as basswood, elm, oak, maple, birch, and aspen. Many birds and animals make their homes in these woodlands.

Ethanol

A fuel made partially from corn. It is used as an alternative to gasoline in automobiles.

Glacier

Huge, slow-moving sheets of ice that grow and shrink as the climate changes. During the Ice Age, some glaciers covered entire regions and measured more than one mile (1.6 km) thick.

Ice Age

An Ice Age occurs when Earth's climate causes a major growth of the polar ice caps, continental ice shelves, and glaciers. The ice sheets can be more than one mile (1.6 km) thick.

Immigrants

People who make a foreign country their home.

Metamorphic Rock

Rocks that change in form because of intense heat and pressure deep in the earth. Gneiss and quartzite are examples of metamorphic rocks.

Mississippi Flyway

Migratory birds, such as ducks and geese, follow routes when they fly south in the fall and north in the spring. The Mississippi Flyway is a major flight corridor that connects the Arctic with the Gulf of Mexico. It generally follows the path of the Mississippi River.

Raptors

Birds of prey that eat meat. Raptors include eagles, falcons, hawks, and owls.

Sedimentary Rock

Rock that is formed by a slow process of pressing together small particles, such as sand, over millions of years.

Voyageurs

French Canadian workers who paddled canoes laden with furs in the 18th and 19th centuries. They paddled long distances through wilderness areas, mainly in Canada and the Upper Midwest. *Voyageur* is a French word that means "traveler."

INDEX